Copyright © 2024 Antionette Barnes All rights reserved

The characters and events portrayed in this book are fictitious. Any similarity to real persons, living or dead, is coincidental and not intended by the author.

No part of this book may be reproduced, or stored in a retrieval system, or transmitted in any form or by any means, electronic, mechanical, photocopying, recording, or otherwise, without express written permission of the publisher.

ISBN: 978-1-7370589-5-3

Printed in the United States of America

Highly Sensitive People:

A book of poems for HSPs

Antionette Barnes

Highly Sensitive People:

A book of poems for HSPs

Table of contents:

1) Hug myself
2) I stand on that
3) Somebody ask me
4) Remind me why I like you
5) Entertain your thoughts
6) Quiet confidence
7) You mean to tell me
8) I'm writing this because
9) The
10) Sensitivity
11) Awareness
12) Around us
13) Facial expression
14) Moods
15) Overwhelmed
16) Deeply feels
17) Under pressure
18) Inward
19) Quiet time
20) Social situations
21) Too sensitive

1 Hug myself

I just had to hug myself
Because I wanted a hug so bad
No,
I needed a hug

I had to hug myself
There was nobody near me to hug
I had to hug myself
I took deep breaths in as I hugged myself

I love myself
I need a companion
But I feel like I'm nowhere close to getting one
Am I close?

Hug myself
I just had to hug myself
At times like this,
I want a deep hug

> "I took deep breaths in as I hugged myself"
>
> —poetic Tamara

WHICH 4 WORDS FROM THE POEM DID YOU SEE FIRST?

C	I	M	V	V	J	O	S
O	F	D	E	E	P	O	B
M	G	C	S	S	F	X	R
P	H	W	W	W	L	R	E
A	I	L	O	V	E	N	A
N	T	T	G	T	S	T	T
I	D	O	U	N	Y	T	H
O	U	U	H	I	M	R	S
N	Z	L	O	V	E	E	U

HUG MYSELF

1. WRITE THE FIRST 4 WORDS HERE.
2. WRITE DOWN WHAT THEY MEAN TO YOU.
3. WRITE DOWN HOW THEY CAN HELP YOU ON YOUR LIFE'S JOURNEY.
4. BE HONEST WITH YOURSELF.

----

2 ▶ I stand on that

I'm not going to keep telling you
Over and over
These words that I have told you once before
Twice before

I stand on that
I stand on what I said
I'm not going to keep repeating myself
I'm not going to take back what I said

Because I stand on that
You should know that
Do you feel where I'm coming from?
Oh, well be it

I stand on that
I stand on my words
I said what I said
Understand me or not

"I'm not going to keep repeating myself"

—*Poetic Tamara*

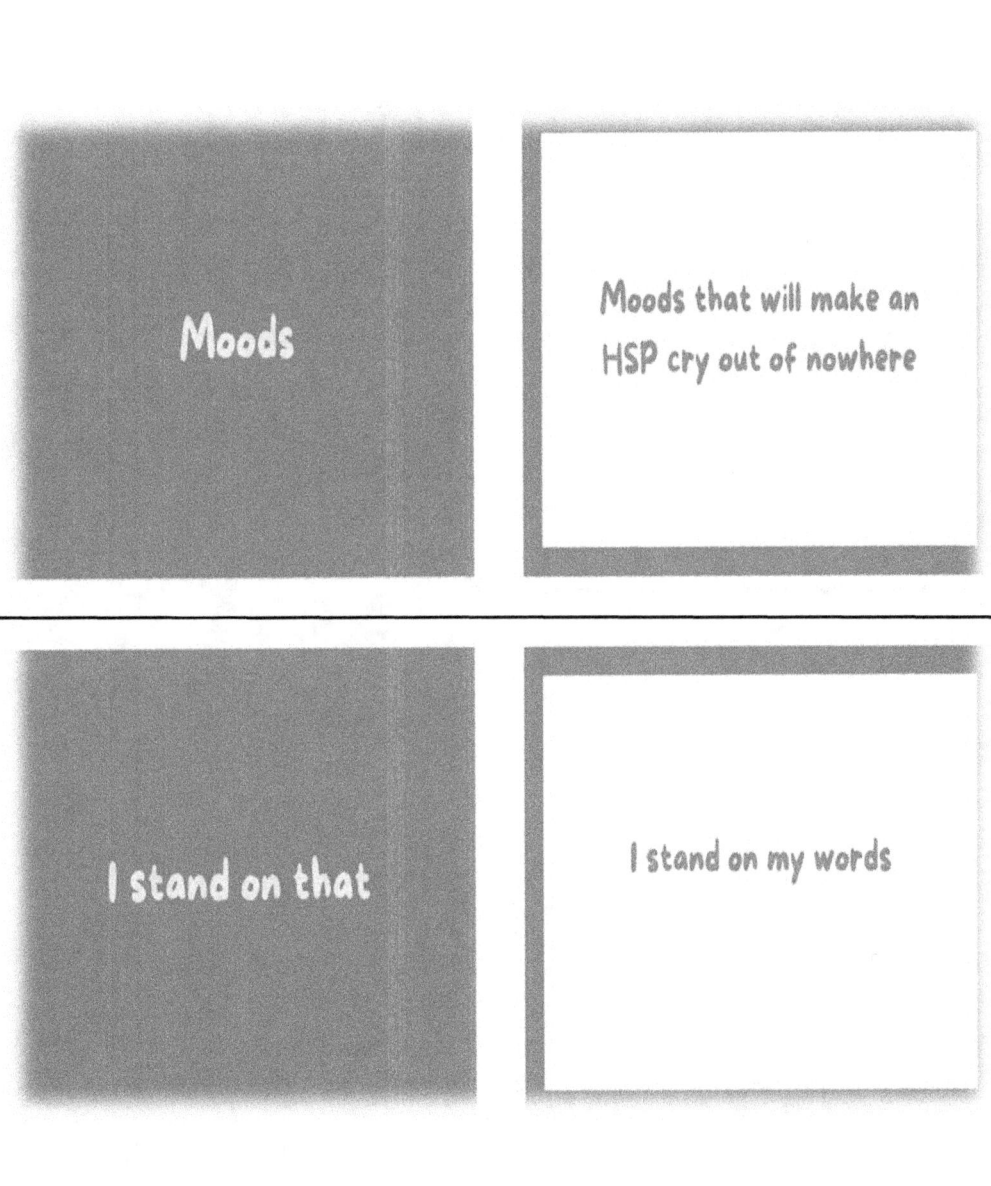

3 ▶ Somebody ask me

Somebody ask me,
How do I feel about being single?
Somebody ask me,
How long have I been single?

Please ask me
So, I can have a deep conversation
About my not-so-much-of-a-love life
So, I can say that, "I wish I have a love life."

Somebody ask me,
To have a deep conversation
I need one
I need help understanding

Understanding why I am single
At night now,
It starts to hit me hard
Sigh!

"So, I can say that, "I wish I have a love life."

—*Poetic Tamara*

4
Remind me why I like you again

I am trying to figure it out
Can't quite put my fingers on it
What is it about you?
Remind me why I like you again

Is it the way you dress?
The way you talk
I know
Maybe it's the way you look at me

Please remind me why I like you again
Surely, I told you
I'm not sure why I like you
We barely spend time together

We don't go out together
Remind me why I like you again
Do you even like me?
Why are you still hanging around here?

> "I'm not sure why I like you"
>
> —Poetic Tamara

5 → Entertain your thoughts

I'm not even going to keep doing this
You do too much
At times, I am wondering
"Why do you think the way that you do?"

I'm not going to entertain your thoughts
Your thoughts are wild
Half the time,
Your thoughts don't be making sense to me

Entertain your thoughts
Not no more
I don't understand what you are saying
Non-sense to me

"your thoughts are wild"
—Poetic Tamara

6 Quiet confidence

I worked on this
For quite some time
Going back and forth
From insecurities

And being hard on myself
To loving myself
Until the day came
For the umpteenth time

That I must change
The way I view myself
I decided
To start with "quiet confidence"

Quiet confidence in my looks
Quiet confidence in my thoughts
Quiet confidence
Until I'm ready to be loud with it

> To start with "quiet confidence"
>
> —Poetic Tamara

WHICH 4 WORDS FROM THE POEM DID YOU SEE FIRST?

Z	S	K	O	O	L	M	T
I	N	S	P	I	R	E	S
W	O	R	K	E	D	P	T
Q	H	O	P	E	E	G	H
U	M	D	E	G	N	E	G
I	X	X	N	I	V	I	U
E	G	A	V	Y	Y	Y	O
T	H	O	O	O	O	P	H
C	L	W	Q	Q	Q	Q	T

QUIET CONFIDENCE

1. WRITE THE FIRST 4 WORDS HERE.
2. WRITE DOWN WHAT THEY MEAN TO YOU.
3. WRITE DOWN HOW THEY CAN HELP YOU ON YOUR LIFE'S JOURNEY.
4. BE HONEST WITH YOURSELF.

---

7 ▶ You mean to tell me

You mean to tell me
That you are mad at me
Because I won't let you
Treat me any kind of way

Do you mean to tell me
That your frustration with me
Is because
I won't let you talk to me recklessly.

You mean to tell me
That your anger is directed at me because
I choose me over you.
I choose my mental health over you

8 ▸ I'm writing this because.....

I'm writing this because

I've came to the realization

That I can sometimes be oversensitive

Large crowds overwhelm me

Loud noises bother me

I can't do stressful situations

I always wanted to be in my quiet place

I tend to find myself deeply thinking

I'm writing this because

I'm not much of a people's person

I pick up on other's emotions

I'm a very emotional person

"That I can sometimes be oversensitive"

—Poetic Tamara

9 The

The not-so-talkative one

The "I love to keep my distance" one

Is in a relationship

But how do they do it?

The "I peep game" one

The "who is all over there" type of person

Is no longer single

Well, what do you know?

"The "who is all over there" type of person"

—Poetic Tamara

10 ▷ Sensitivity

Highly sensitive people

Can be extra sensitive

Which might be seen as a sign of weakness

Instead of a sign of strengths

Sensitivity

Could look like

Feelings are hurt

Which might be because they feel deeply

Sensitivity

Could be seen

As a state of vulnerability

Which might cause them to withdraw into a flight state

"Which might be because they feel deeply"

—*Poetic Tamara*

11 ▸ Awareness

Keen awareness

To other people's feelings

To what's going on around the way

Fully aware

Awareness

Of one's own feelings

To one's own actions

Trying to inner stand what's within

WHICH 4 WORDS FROM THE POEM DID YOU SEE FIRST?

U	H	A	P	P	Y	S	S
T	A	E	R	G	N	G	S
N	K	R	S	I	F	N	E
O	O	P	H	E	U	I	N
T	J	T	C	R	L	L	E
G	I	B	Y	A	L	E	R
W	C	J	J	W	Y	E	A
G	D	I	D	A	V	F	W
A	C	T	I	O	N	S	A

AWARENESS

1. WRITE THE FIRST 4 WORDS HERE.
2. WRITE DOWN WHAT THEY MEAN TO YOU.
3. WRITE DOWN HOW THEY CAN HELP YOU ON YOUR LIFE'S JOURNEY.
4. BE HONEST WITH YOURSELF.

----

12 Around us

There should be positive people around us
So, our energy won't be drained
Bashful talking
Keep that a minimum around us

Small crowds should be
Around us mainly
Places to go recharge
Should be around us

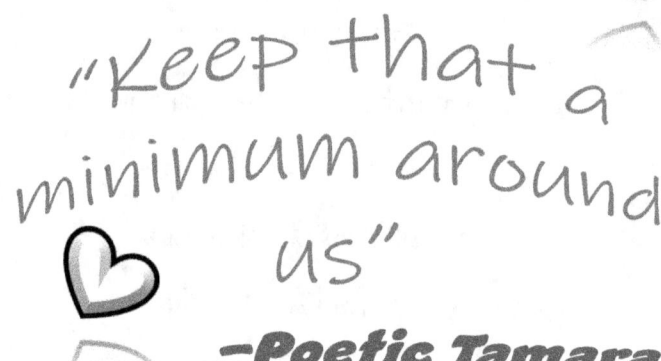
"Keep that a minimum around us"
—Poetic Tamara

 Facial expressions

They might not say it but
They will wear it
It will be written all over
Their faces

HSPs
Can pick up on it
They can read
Facial expressions

HSPs
Can pick up a person's emotion
Based on their
Facial expression

> "They will wear it"
>
> —Poetic Tamara

# 14 Moods

Certain moods affect them

It's not like they want the moods

To affect them

It just happens

Out of nowhere

Moods after moods

Different kinds of moods

Moods that will make an HSP cry out of nowhere

♡ "OUT OF NOWHERE" ♡
—POETIC TAMARA

 Overwhelmed

Oh my,
This is something that we dislike
The feeling of being overwhelmed
We need time

Space is a must
With being overwhelmed
Requires time and space to recharge
Overwhelmed....

Breathe deeply
Air it out
Overwhelmed....
We have to learn to cool down

> "Requires time and space to recharge"
>
> —Poetic Tamara

| Overwhelmed | Space is a must |
| Deeply Feels | They could think it's a weakness |

16 Deeply feels

One thing about HSPs,
They feel differently
When I say differently
I mean they deeply feel

They could think it's a weakness
To the heart,
Is what they might take of what people say
By being able to deeply feel

Other people's emotions are what they take on
Being emotional is what some might feel
By deeply feeling,
They can put themselves in other people's position

 **Under pressure**

Highly sensitive people
Work on this one thing,
Being under pressure
When tough times come,

It's not time to feel under pressure
Work through that feeling
Or take a break
While being under pressure

Means y'all don't have to break down
Y'all are strong
Overcome being under pressure
Y'all got this

WHICH 4 WORDS FROM THE POEM DID YOU SEE FIRST?

P	R	E	S	S	U	R	E
C	P	U	U	G	O	B	L
L	E	W	B	N	N	A	C
V	T	I	R	E	D	Q	Z
K	P	T	E	O	M	E	M
R	H	O	A	D	X	X	R
O	K	U	K	F	E	E	L
W	R	G	D	R	E	A	M
X	T	H	P	O	Y	E	K

UNDER PRESSURE

1. WRITE THE FIRST 4 WORDS HERE.
2. WRITE DOWN WHAT THEY MEAN TO YOU.
3. WRITE DOWN HOW THEY CAN HELP YOU ON YOUR LIFE'S JOURNEY.
4. BE HONEST WITH YOURSELF.

----

18 ➤ Inward

I have learned
To go inward
When I go inward,
I can calm myself down

By going inward,
I can sit with my thoughts
I can find answers that I seek
Going inwards means inner monologue

> "Going inwards means inner monologue."
>
> —Poetic Tamara

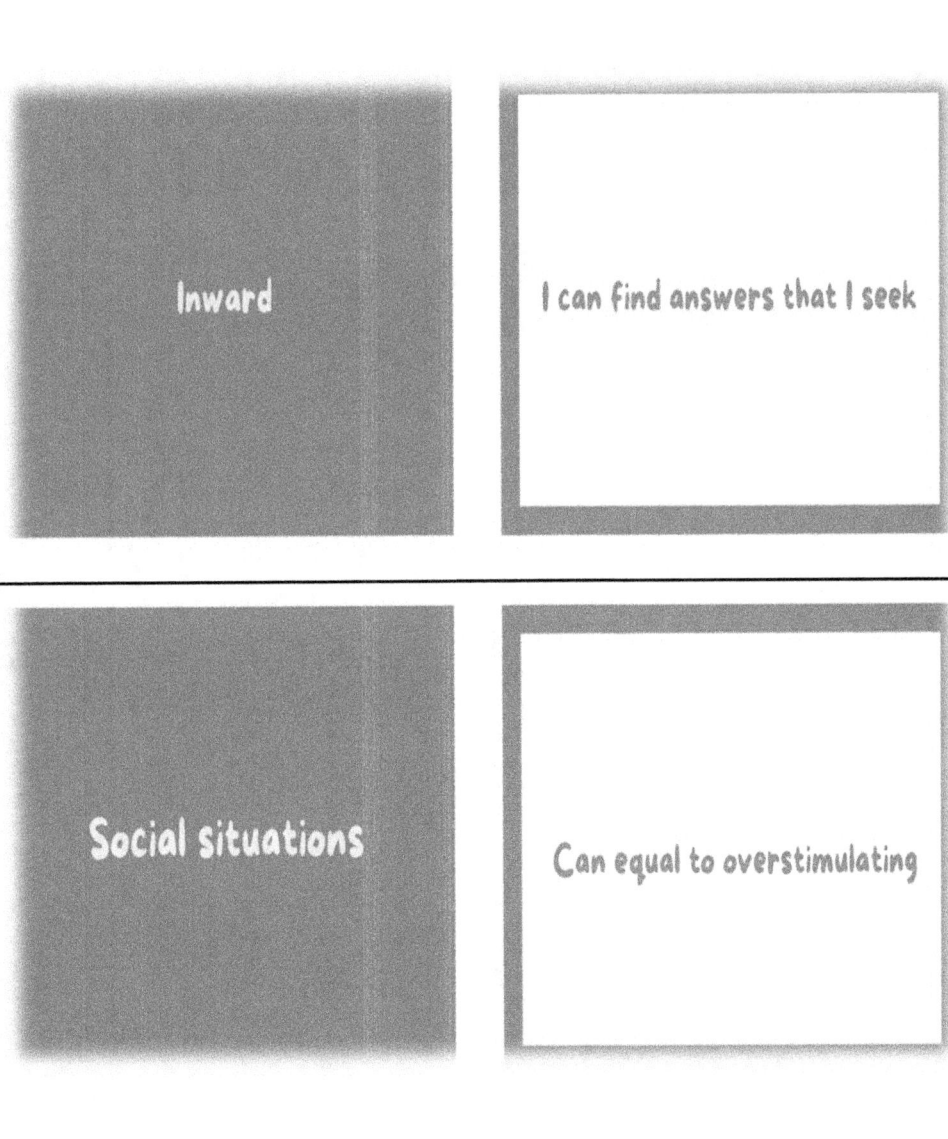

19 Quiet time

There is nothing wrong
With a little quiet time
Here and now
Every so often

Quiet time can be helpful
See quiet time as being meaningful
Use your quiet time to get back to you
Enjoy your quiet time while you can

With quiet time,
Comes time to shake back
A time to be at peace with yourself
Use your quiet time wisely

"Use your quiet time to get back to you."

—POETIC TAMARA

 Social situations

Social situations
Where do I begin?
I will start somewhere
They can be overwhelming

Social situations
Can equal to overstimulating
HSP will need
A chance to get away

If the social situations
Are large gatherings
It's just the way they are
With certain social situations

> "Can equal to overstimulating."
> —POETIC TAMARA

21 Too sensitive

At times,
I feel like
I'm too sensitive
More sensitive

Then the norm
Being too sensitive
Is what I took
As a sign of weakness

Too sensitive because
I cry sometimes out of nowhere
When someone talks to me
Or how certain things get said to me

Too sensitive	At times
I'm writing this because....	I always wanted to be in my quiet place

Answer Keys:

WHICH 4 WORDS FROM THE POEM DID YOU SEE FIRST?

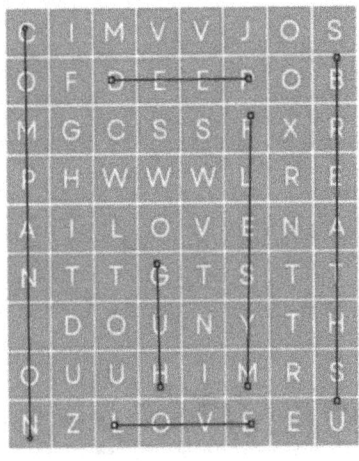

HUG MYSELF

WHICH 4 WORDS FROM THE POEM DID YOU SEE FIRST?

QUIET CONFIDENCE

WHICH 4 WORDS FROM THE POEM DID YOU SEE FIRST?

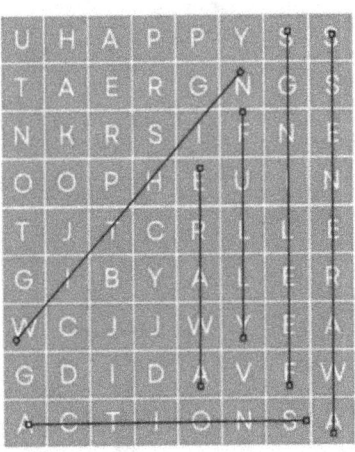

AWARENESS

WHICH 4 WORDS FROM THE POEM DID YOU SEE FIRST?

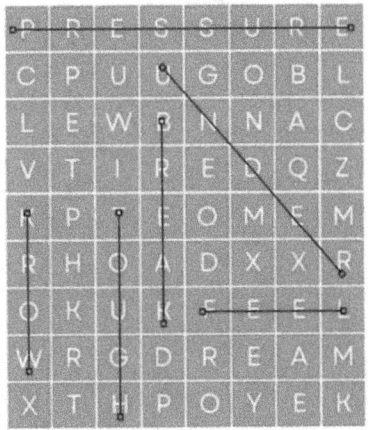

UNDER PRESSURE

Don't forget the introverts

By: Antionette Barnes

Don't forget the introverts

Table of contents:

1) Do introverts get into relationships?
2) What do introverts do in relationships?
3) Writing is therapy
4) Poetic love
5) I don't want to be bothered
6) I don't try hard
7) Self-questioning
8) No rush at all
9) Quiet my thoughts
10) Do you need a hug?
11) Small talk
12) A need for
13) Feel anything or feel nothing
14) In stillness
15) Lack
16) A need to recharge
17) Drain
18) Speak up
19) Prefers
20) Spotlight

Do introverts get into relationships?

This is a question to ponder
Not sure if it's a tough question
But someone answer, please
Do introverts get into relationships?

To be honest,
I'm asking
For myself
I'm what one would consider an introvert

Do introverts get into relationships?
I learned to love my isolation
I'm considered a highly sensitive person
And I be needing to recharge

> "I'm what one will consider an introvert"
> —Poetic Tamara

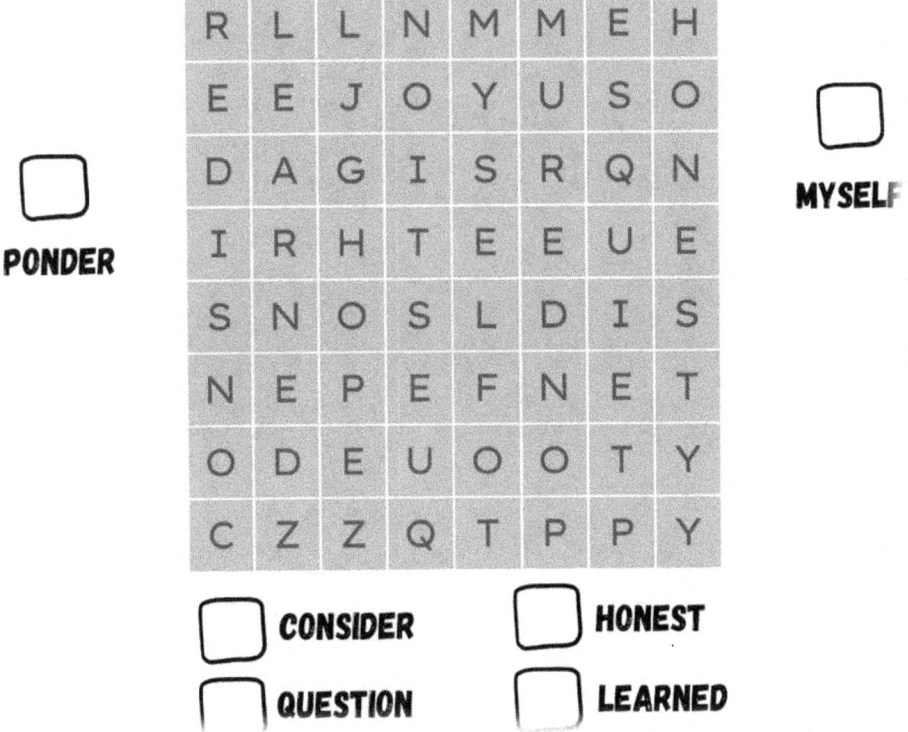

Draw your own poem:

2
What do introverts do in relationships?

So, tell me
what do introverts do in relationships?
They're not the talkative type
Well, not around certain people

Introverts
Love their alone time
Introverts
Are not the type to strike up conversations

What do introverts do in relationships?
Off standish personality
Daydreamers who be all in their thoughts
Are some of the qualities that might make it hard for relationships

"Love their alone time"

—Poetic Tamara

Writing is therapy

Outlet,

I don't have many choices

Therapy,

I found therapy in writing

So, for me

Writing is therapy

Writing is my outlet

If you won't listen to me

Can you please read my words?

Writing is therapy

Writing is healing

Writing is a form of impression

"Can you please read my words?"

—Poetic Tamara

Writing is therapy

Can you please read my words?
Writing is therapy
Writing is healing
Writing is a form of impression

I didn't try hard

Once I saw,
What I needed to see
Once I heard,
What I needed to hear

Quiet my thoughts

Quiet
Thoughts
I'm trying to concentrate here
Focus

Small talk

This can be a hard thing
For a person who
Don't fool with a lot of people
Who loves to cut to the chase

Poetic love

The type of love that I want
Is a beautiful type of love
The type of love that will have
Me falling in love over and over again

That's what I call
A poetic love
Is it true
That introverts can fall in love too?

I want to keep getting
Butterflies from my love
Poetic love
Pure poetic love

"Is a beautiful type of love."

—Poetic Tamara

I don't want to be bothered

It's the introvert in me
Don't take it to the heart
It's just that
I don't want to be bothered

Don't talk to me
Don't look at me
Don't bother to hit me up later on
I don't want to be bothered

> "It's the introvert in me"
>
> —Poetic Tamara

I didn't try hard

I didn't try hard
To win him over
I didn't try hard
At all

Once I saw,
What I needed to see
Once I heard,
What I needed to hear

I stopped
I stopped trying
To be with him
I didn't try hard

"What I needed to see"
-Poetic Tamara

Self-questioning

I started doing this a lot now
Even more than before
I am going through something
In my life yet again

Self-questioning
I have been asking myself a lot of questions
Self-questioning myself
About myself

Self-questioning about my life
I still have not figured out my purpose
I still have not accomplished my goals
I have been asking myself, "Why am I here?"

"I have been asking myself a lot of questions"
—Poetic Tamara

WORD SEARCH: MARK THE BOXES

SELF-QUESTIONING

S	T	A	R	T	E	D	P
H	F	Z	F	L	E	S	U
G	D	I	I	P	S	G	R
U	R	E	G	W	A	A	P
O	E	E	N	U	J	J	O
R	A	F	S	N	R	O	S
H	M	I	O	M	F	E	E
T	G	L	B	L	H	K	D

☐ STARTED ☐ FIGURED

☐ THROUGH ☐ SELF
☐ LIFE ☐ PURPOSE

Draw your own poem:

No rush at all

There's no rush at all
well, there shouldn't be
Take your time
Make sure to get things right

What's the rushing for?
No rush at all
Your plans will fall into place
when the right time presents itself

"Make sure to get things right"

—Poetic Tamara

Quiet my thoughts

It be hard to quiet my thoughts
There be so much
Running through my head
Replaying over and over

Quiet

Thoughts

I'm trying to concentrate here

Focus

"I'm trying to concentrate here"

—Poetic Tamara

Do you need a hug?

What's wrong?

Why the face?

That frown

Is turned the wrong way

Do you need a hug?

I sense that something is off

You are not yourself

Do you need a hug?

It's okay to feel how you feel

It's okay to be yourself

Did somebody say something wrong to you?

Do you need a hug?

> "I sense that something is off"
>
> —Poetic Tamara

Small talk

This can be a hard thing

For a person who

Don't fool with a lot of people

Who loves to cut to the chase

Small talk?

For them

Small talk can be a waste of time

Especially if they don't feel like talking

"Small talk can be a waste of time."

—Poetic Tamara

A need for

A need for alone time

A need for quiet time

A need for self-care

A need for self-check-in

A need for meaningful conversations

A need for genuine love

A need for self-love

A need for hugs

> "A need for meaningful conversations."
> —Poetic Tamara

Feel anything or feel nothing

Feel anything or feel nothing

Words?

They can hurt

How am I supposed to feel?

Feel anything or feel nothing

Social life?

What social life?

I barely like to talk

Feel anything or feel nothing

Love?

Numb

How does love really feel like?

"How does love really feel like?"

—Poetic Tamara

WORD SEARCH: MARK THE BOXES

FEEL ANYTHING OR FEEL NOTHING

C	T	H	O	M	B	G	A
A	O	U	N	Z	N	L	A
R	H	R	E	I	L	L	N
E	I	T	H	E	Q	U	H
Y	I	T	E	Z	M	D	Y
O	O	F	P	B	Q	D	Y
N	B	M	S	D	R	O	W
A	N	Y	T	H	I	N	G

☐ WORDS ☐ HURT ☐ FEEL ☐ ANYTHING ☐ NOTHING ☐ NUMB

Draw your own poem:

In stillness

In stillness,

Is where you can find yourself

In stillness,

Is where you can think of "What could go right?"

In stillness,

You can really listen

In stillness,

A state of calmness can come about

"A state of calmness can come about."

—Poetic Tamara

Lack

Introverts

Don't lack feelings

They are individuals

Who feel deeply

Being an introvert

Don't mean that they

Lack social skills

Large groups make them uneasy

Introverts

Don't lack leadership

They have great leadership skills

In that they are great listeners and goal oriented

"Large groups make them uneasy."

—Poetic Tamara

WORD SEARCH: MARK THE BOXES

LACK

S	G	N	I	L	E	E	F
Y	O	U	G	R	E	A	T
Y	I	N	S	P	I	R	E
S	M	O	T	I	V	E	T
A	H	L	A	C	K	G	J
E	H	Z	J	W	B	B	B
N	S	K	I	L	L	S	M
U	K	Y	S	L	A	O	G

☐ SKILLS ☐ GOALS

☐ LACK ☐ UNEASY

☐ FEELINGS ☐ GREAT

Draw your own poem:

16
A need to recharge

I can personally say
That I experience this
Many a time
A need to recharge

I be needing
A need to recharge often
Recharge from my day
Recharge from conversations

A need to recharge
To be left with myself
A need to recharge
To think things over

> "Recharge from conversations."
>
> —Poetic Tamara

Drain

Drain after conversations

Drain when the day is over

Drain when people leave

Drain after I leave

Drain alone

Drain around people

Drain even after I wake up

Drain....

"Drain around people."
—Poetic Tamara

Speak up

Don't be afraid

Dear ones

This is nothing

To shy away from

If you speak up

You will be voicing your opinions

You shouldn't be afraid

To speak up

Speak up when you need to

Speak up when you want to

Speak up when you are bothered

Be mindful of how you feel when you speak up

"Be mindful of how you feel when you speak up."

—Poetic Tamara

A need to recharge

A need to recharge
To be left with myself
A need to recharge
To think things over

In stillness

In stillness,
You can really listen
In stillness,
A state of calmness can come about

Do you need a hug?

Do you need a hug?
I sense that something is off
You are not yourself
Do you need a hug?

Speak up

Speak up when you need to
Speak up when you want to
Speak up when you are bothered
Be mindful of how you feel when you speak up

Prefers

Prefers,

Laidback over fast-paced

Meaningful conversations over small talk

Mainly alone time then group time

Quiet time then social time

Prefers,

To hold their emotions then express them

Texts over phone calls

Time to recharge then to keep going

Tend to avoid conflicts instead of facing them

"Hold their emotions then express them."

—Poetic Tamara

Spotlight

I can speak

Openly on this

I'm an introvert

Who doesn't like the spotlight

Attention on me?

I shy away from it

I don't like the spotlight

Center of attention?

All focus on me

I get so nervous

I must get this together

But....

"Attention on me?"
—Poetic Tamara

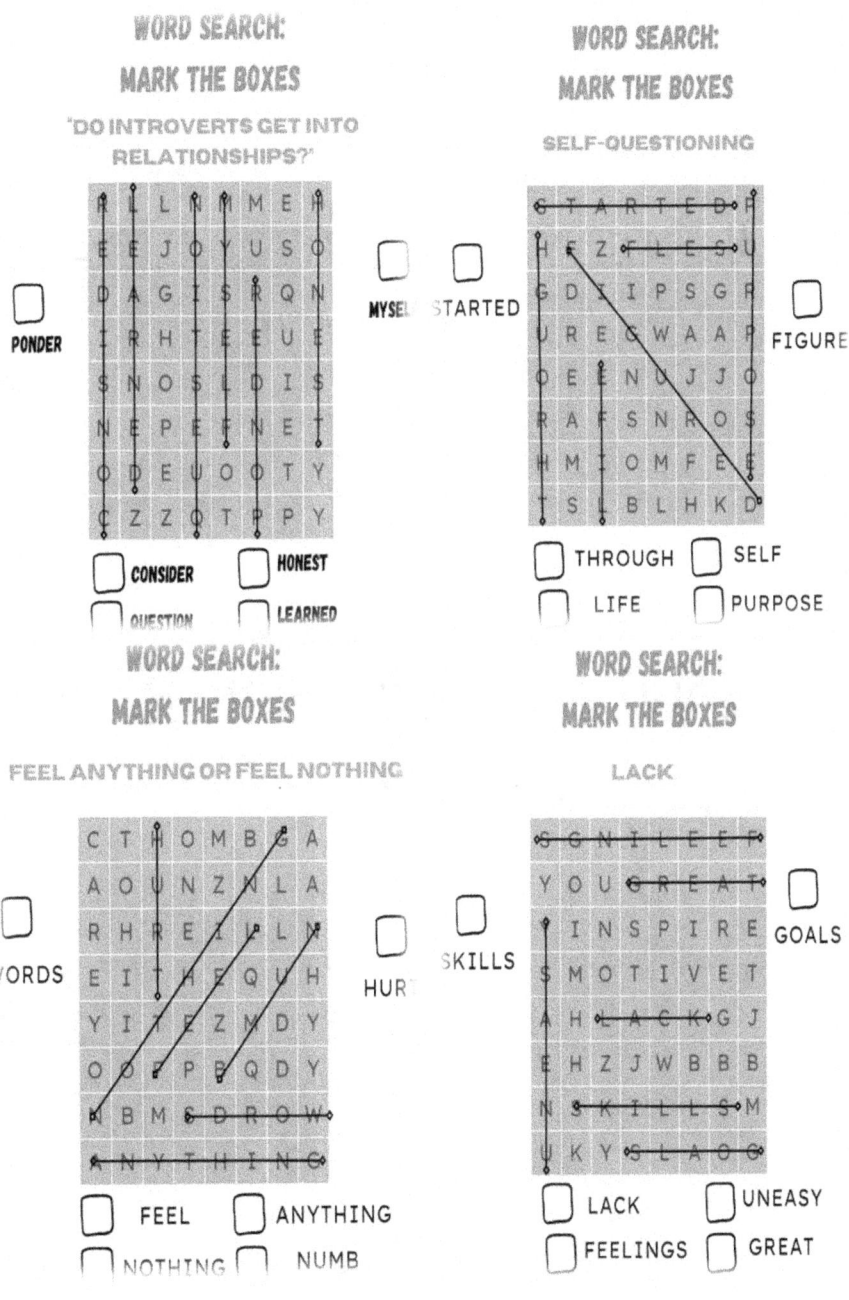

Other books by Antionette Barnes:

- Poetry From The Heart
- Numb to this single life: A collection of poems for all of the single folks
- Leave me to my thoughts
- Going against yourself

Journal by Antionette Barnes:

- Unlock What's Deep Inside: An Affirmation Journal